FRONT COVER: Artistic rendering of Guitarist playing an electric guitar

Fastlines: The Combined Cassette and Booklet Tutor

Cassette (mp3s) and Documentation

Copyright 2016 GMI - Guitar & Music Institute

ISBN 978-0-9956732-0-5

All Rights Reserved

No part of this book or mp3s may be reprinted, or reproduced, or utilised in any form by electronic, mechanical or other means, now known or hereafter invented, including photocopying and recording, or in any information or retrieval system, without the written permission of the publisher.

Music composed and recorded by Ged Brockie

Gary Fimister - Bass and Dave Stewart - Drums

Recording and mixdown at K.S.M. Recording Studios- Edinburgh

Music typeset by G.B. Guitar & Music Institute

Graphic Design by Chris Donaldson

Proof reading by Douglas Urquhart

TABLE OF CONTENTS

FOREWORD..4

FASTLINES...5

FASTLINES SOLO...14

BACKING TRACKS...16

PROJECTS..22

QR CODES..25

DOWNLOAD YOUR AUDIO FILES..31

PLEASE REVIEW THIS BOOK..32

FOREWORD FROM GED BROCKIE

Thank you for purchasing Fastlines Blues Guitar Method Primer, a work that first saw the light of day back in the early 1990's and through digital technology has now been re designed and re published for a new generation of guitarists. This is the first of three blues tutors in the Fastlines range which in total consists of nine books in total.

Each Fastlines blues packages leads the guitarist from the ideas presented here to more challenging ideas in later books. I'd encourage you to try out these other publications when you feel ready to do so.

I have had the joy of performing, teaching and studying the guitar throughout my life. I feel, now more than ever, the pursuit of expression through music and the arts in general can be a transformational experience and a much needed counterweight to the immediacy of the Internet world we now live in.

I created Fastlines so that people could work from a collection of musical ideas that they could use in improvised solo situations. Coming up with lines that make musical sense is one of the great challenges when improvising and that is how the Fastlines concept was born. As well as this, I wanted to provide an understanding of how each line functioned. Through this understanding, lines could be altered and changed to fit various harmonic scenarios. The short solo that is included in this book offers the student insight into ways in which different lines can be joined together to create a meaningful improvisation. Backing tracks give context for each of the memorised lines to be realised and heard against and finally, the projects allow for long term development of the lines presented here.

I hope you enjoy using this work and that you will consider the other books in the series which were developed over a two year period. I am confident that they will bring you a deeper understanding of the jazz genre and help you meet your improvisational goals.

Ged Brockie

Ged Brockie has performed in almost every conceivable musical scenario over a thirty year period. His own band recordings comprise his own compositions, arrangements and performance with some of Scotland's finest musicians (The Mirror's Image - Circular Records 2009, The Last View From Mary's Place - Circular Records 2004). He was one of the main writers in the Scottish Guitar Quartet (SGQ) recording three albums (Near The Circle 2001, Fait Accompli 2003, Landmarks 2005) touring across Europe to critical acclaim. The DVD "Five Innovations For Guitar & Orchestra - Circular Records 2011" featured Ged with a twenty one piece orchestra. He has also worked with the RSNO, OSO, Carl Davis, Hummie Mann, West End shows on tour, TV & radio, music industry events, all levels of music education from high school to university and has a wide range of compositions used in film, TV and media.

Ged is the lead instructor and driving force behind GMI and guides the programs of learning within it.

www.gedbrockie.com

FASTLINES

FASTLINES Blues Primer

FASTLINE 1

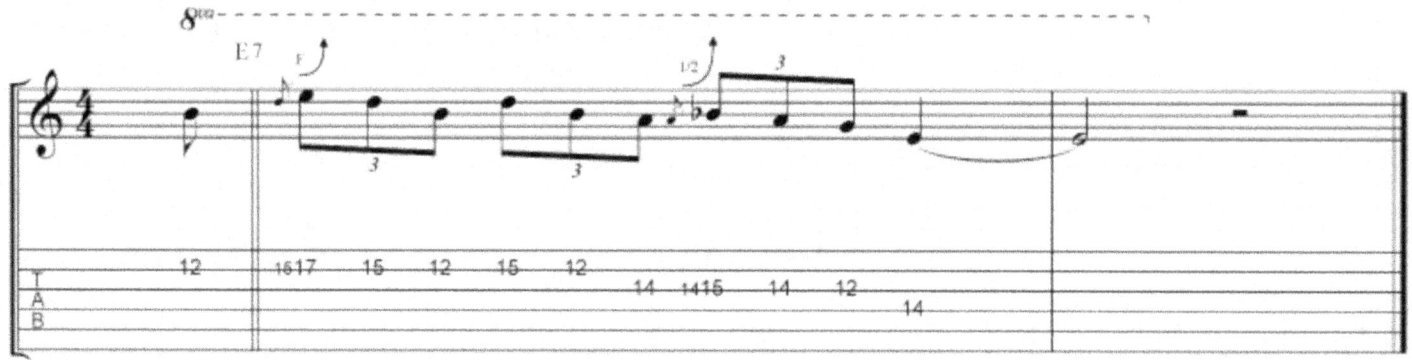

FASTLINE One Tempo: 70
Scale used: E blues scale.
Tech./harmonic aspects: Full/half-tone bends
Comments:
1. This Fastline includes examples of full and half-tone bends. When playing bends, always use one or two of the remaining lower fingers to help support the finger that is executing the bend. In this example both bends are played by the third finger of the left hand with the second finger providing support. Using this support technique gives you more control and makes string bending much easier. Always listen carefully while playing bends to make sure that they are in tune.

FASTLINE 2

FASTLINE Two Tempo: 70
Scale used: A minor pentatonic.
Tech./harmonic aspects: Vibrato
Comments:
1. Here we see vibrato being applied to a note that has been bent up by a tone. This is an essential blues guitar technique. To achieve vibrato with a bend, first bend the note the specified distance (in this example a tone). At the apex of the bend release slightly. This is immediately followed by bending the string back to it's full tone bend position. Repeating this maneuver for the duration of the note will result in vibrato being applied to the string.

FASTLINE 3

FASTLINE Three Tempo: 90
Scale used: A pentatonic minor.
Tech./harmonic aspects: Quarter-tone bends
Comments:
1. Blues guitar playing is very vocal in style and includes many vocal inflections. The quarter tone bend shown in this example is a very common device and when applied, adds a vocal quality to the line. The quarter tone bend is played by bending a note half the distance of a half tone bend. Once the desired distance is reached it is important to dampen (silence) the note so that you do not hear the not return to its original pitch. Dampen the note by lightly releasing the pressure of the finger playing the note.

FASTLINE 4

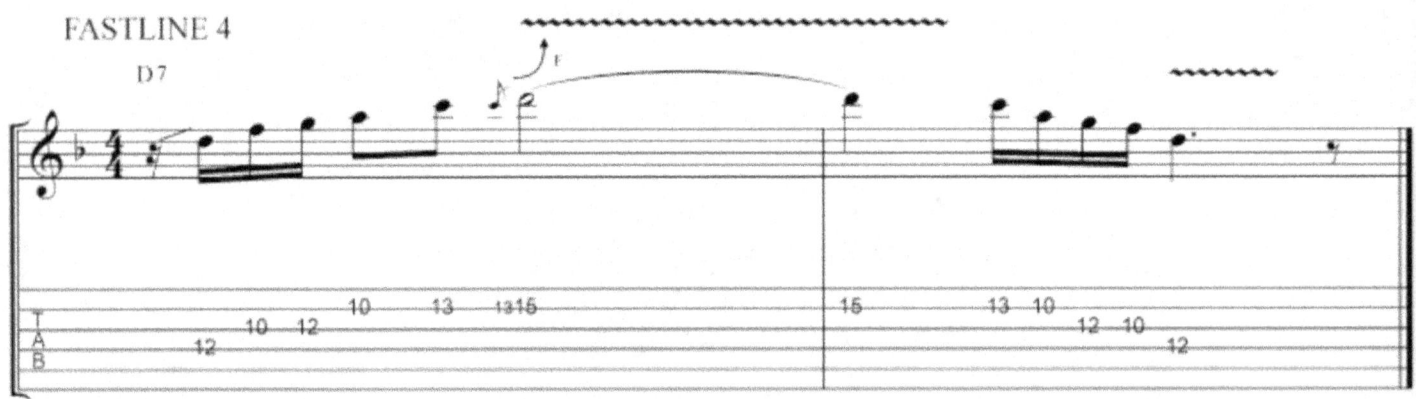

FASTLINE Four Tempo: 68
Scale used: D pentatonic minor.
Tech./harmonic aspects: Vibrato, full-tone bends
Comments:
1. Vibrato is widely used in blues and a good grasp of this technique is essential. There are three main types of vibrato available to the guitarist, one of which is shown in this Fastline (the other two are discussed in the intermediate and advanced Fastline packs). The vibrato in this Fastline is played by bending and returning the note to it's original pitch. The "width" of the vibrato in relation to the guitar neck is determined by the distance of the bend and the speed is determined by how quickly the note is bent and released.

FASTLINE 5

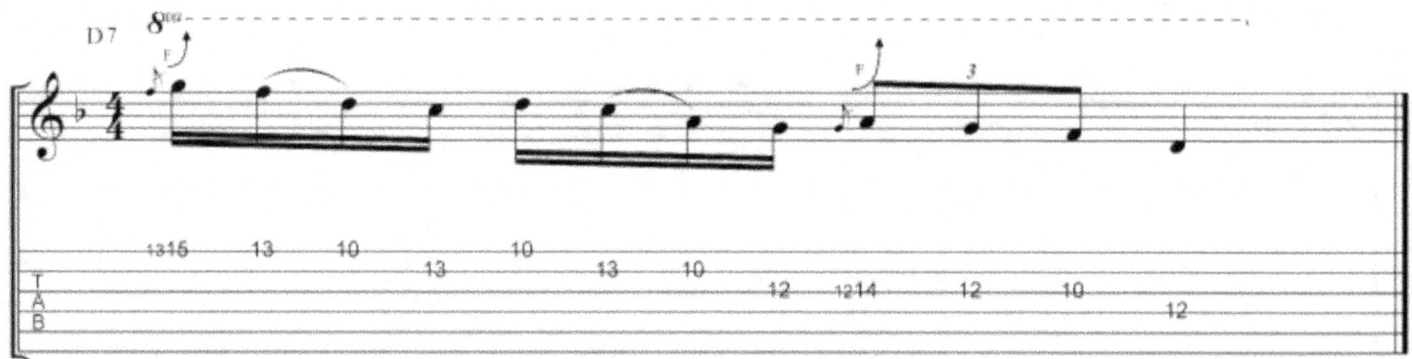

FASTLINE Five   Tempo: 70
Scale used: D pentatonic minor.
Tech./harmonic aspects: Full-tone bends, pull-offs.
Comments:
1. This line contains all the techniques covered in the first four Fastlines.

FASTLINE 6

FASTLINE Six   Tempo: 72
Scale used: A pentatonic minor.
Tech./harmonic aspects: Staccato, vibrato, quarter-tone bends.
Comments:
1. Fastline six includes some staccato (detached) phrasing. The stacatto notes are the first three notes in the first bar. Detach these notes by either damping each note (as in Fastline three), after it is picked, or by lightly resting on the string with the pick therefore stopping the string vibrating.

FASTLINE 7

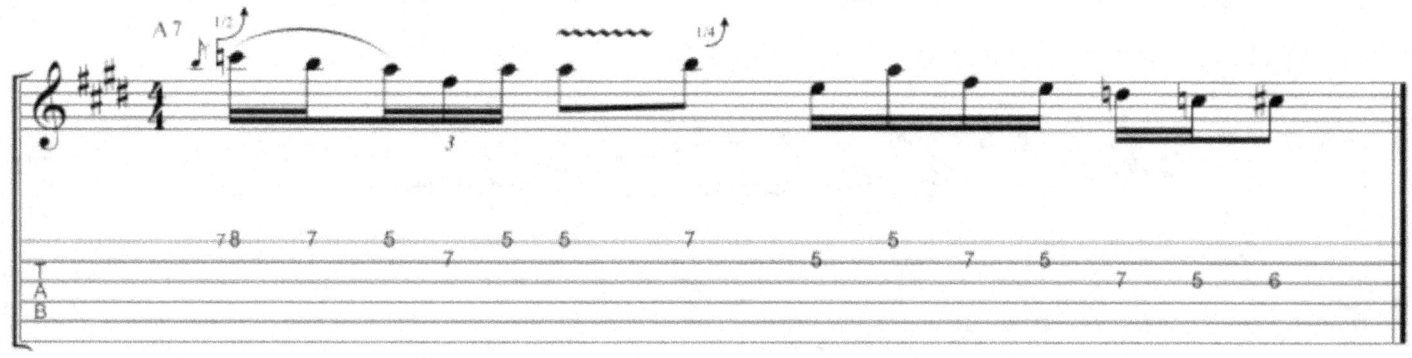

FASTLINE Seven   Tempo: 62
Scale used: C sharp pentatonic minor.
Tech./harmonic aspects: Vibrato, full/half-tone bends.
Comments:
1. In this Fastline there is a slow bend that stops before reaching its destination and which does not return to its original pitch. Start this bend as explained in Fastline one, as it reaches its peak, dampen the string as in Fastline number three.

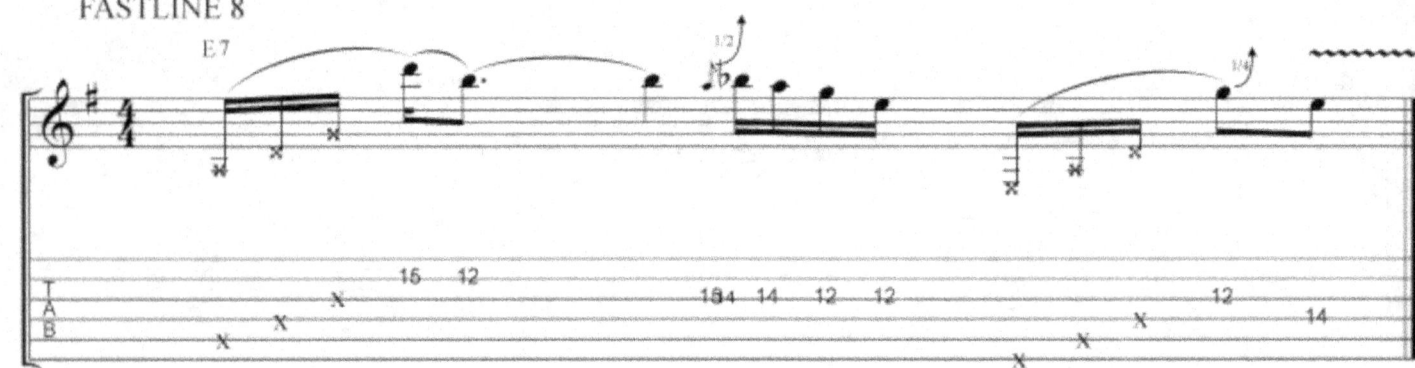

FASTLINE Eight   Tempo: 74

Scale used: E pentatonic minor.
Tech./harmonic aspects: Rake, vibrato, half/quarter-tone bends.
Comments:
1. String raking is a percussive technique that involves the muting of strings. To mute a string, lightly rest the heel of your right hand on the strings near the bridge of the guitar, then sweep pick (constant downward motion with pick) through the designated strings as shown above.
2. This line also includes a common blues rhythmic figure on the first beat of the bar (semi-quaver/dotted quaver

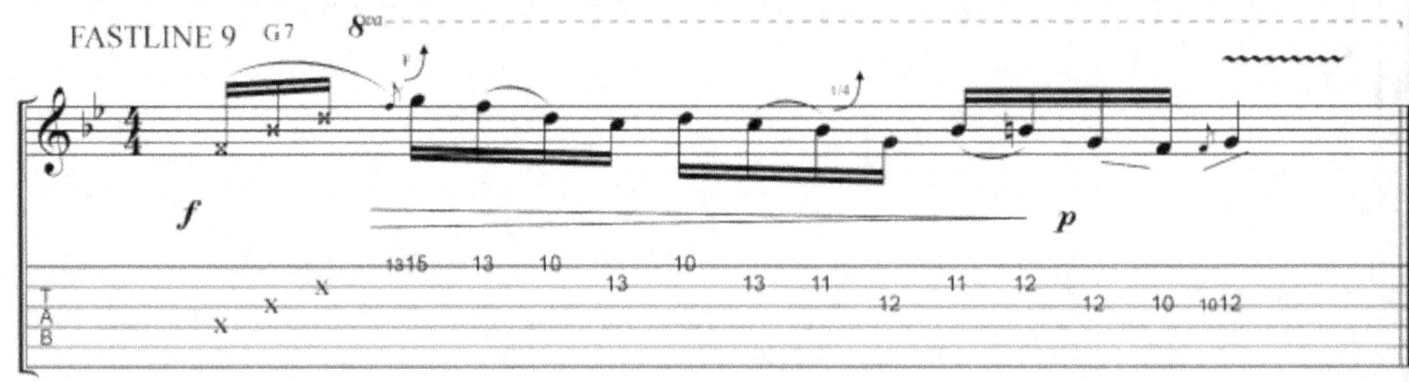

FASTLINE Nine   Tempo: 70

Scale used: G pentatonic minor.
Tech./harmonic aspects: Rake, vibrato, full/quarter-tone bends.
Comments:
1. Here we have an example of applying dynamics (volume changes) to a line. Note how the line starts off loud (forte), then gets steadily quieter (decrescendo), finally finishing quietly (pianissimo).

FASTLINE Ten   Tempo: 80

Scale used: D blues.
Tech./harmonic aspects: Full-tone bends, slides.
Comments:
1. This is another example of dynamics being applied to a line.

FASTLINE 11

FASTLINE Eleven   Tempo: 92
Scale used: B blues.
Tech./harmonic aspects: Minor third bend
Comments:
1. Fastline eleven includes an example of a minor third bend (three frets). Approach this bend in the same manner as the tone and half-tone bends in Fastline one. Note, lighter strings make this bend much easier to play!

FASTLINE 12

FASTLINE Twelve   Tempo: 100
Scale used: E pentatonic minor.
Tech./harmonic aspects: Full tone bends, slow bends, vibrato.
Comments:
1. Riffs are a commonly used device in blues improvisation. A riff is a repeated rhythmic and melodic figure. In this line the riff consists of four triplets found in bar one which are then repeated in the third bar. The last triplet figure of the riff, in bar three, is slightly modified as a lead into the last note of the line.
2. The full tone bend on the first quaver of each triplet group is cut at it's apex and does not return back to the original "D" note.
3. Cut the note by "damping" it as described in Fastline three.

FASTLINE 13

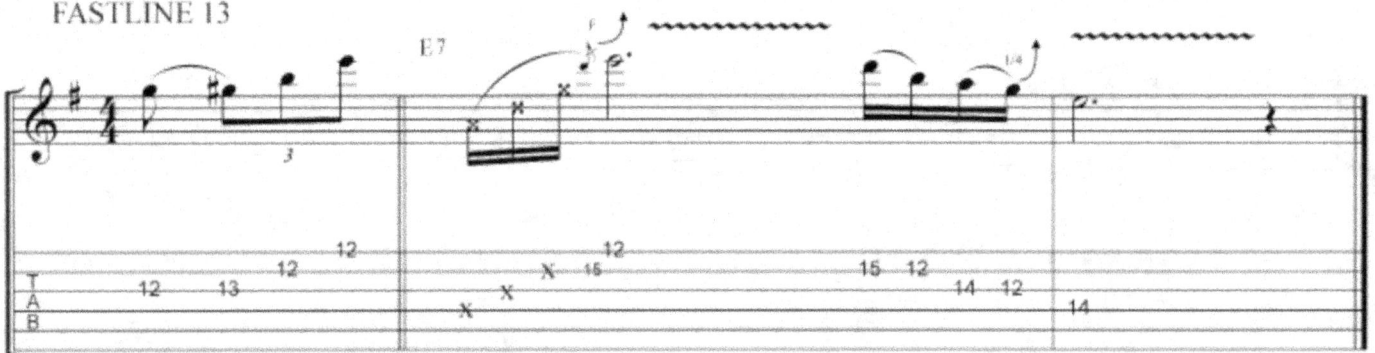

FASTLINE Thirteen Tempo: 126
Scale used: E pentatonic minor.
Tech./harmonic aspects: Full and quarter-tone bends, rake, vibrato, slurring.
Comments:
1. This line opens with a stand blues rhythmic/melodic figure. This figure usually starts on the second half of the third beat (as in this example) comprising of a quaver followed by a triplet.

FASTLINE 14

FASTLINE Fourteen Tempo: 96
Scale used: E pentatonic minor.
Tech./harmonic aspects: Slide, Full/half tone bend, slurring.
Comments:
1. Fastline fourteen starts with a slide (glissando). Begin the slide two or three notes lower than the first notated note. Pick the note that the slide starts on, do not pick the starting note of the line.
2. The figure described in the previous Fastline occurs on the second half of the bar.

FASTLINE 15

FASTLINE Fifteen Tempo: 130
Scale used: C sharp pentatonic minor.
Tech./harmonic aspects: Full tone bends.
Comments:
1. This Fastline includes an example of a common rhythmic device found in blues guitar. It is a three note riff played in straight quavers. Playing the riff with this rhythm implies three against four syncopated pattern because of the shifting of the accents.

FASTLINE 16

FASTLINE Sixteen Tempo: 108
Scale used: E blues.
Tech./harmonic aspects: Slides, slurring, quarter tone bends.
Comments:
1. This line contains the technique of slurring onto open strings of the guitar. Play the last two notes of the line (open B and E strings) with the second and third fingers of your right hand. This avoids an awkward string skip.

FASTLINE 17

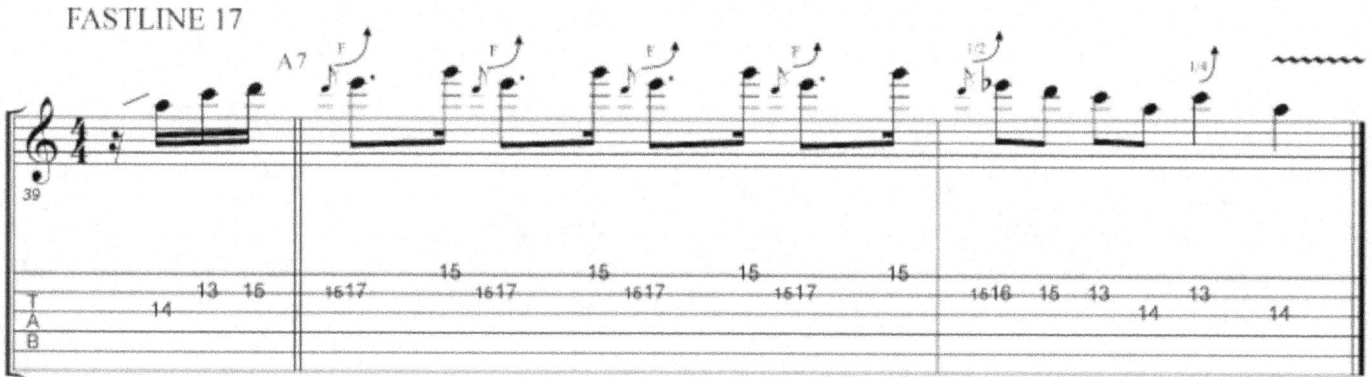

FASTLINE Seventeen Tempo: 76
Scale used: A blues.
Tech./harmonic aspects: Vibrato, full/half/quarter tone bends, slides.
Comments:
1. Keep the fourth finger of the left hand on the G note for the whole of the first bar while repeatedly bending the D on the B string up a tone.

FASTLINE 18

FASTLINE Eighteen Tempo: 106
Scale used: C blues.
Tech./harmonic aspects: Slow bend, rake, quarter tone bend, vibrato, slurring.
Comments:
1. Place a small barre across the B and E strings with your first finger to play to play the first two notes of this line.

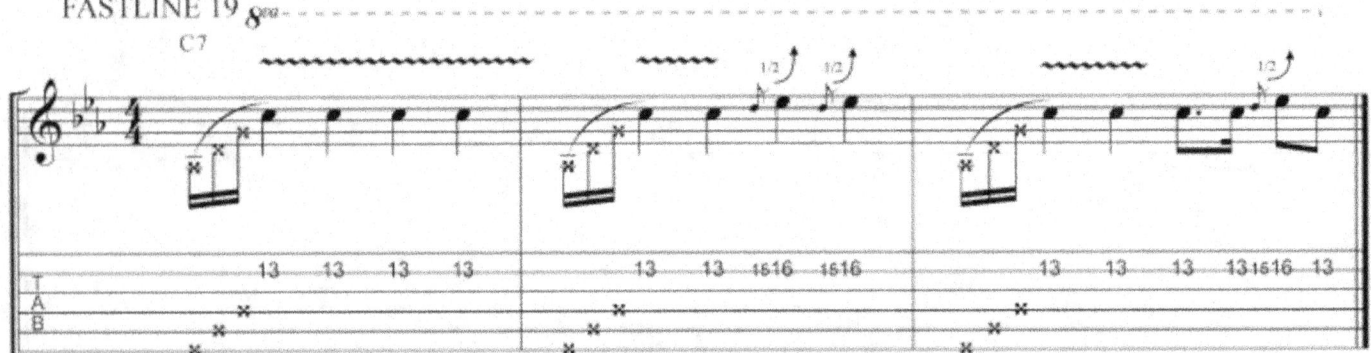

FASTLINE Nineteen Tempo: 126
Scale used: C major.
Tech./harmonic aspects: Rakes, half tone bends, vibrato.
Comments:
1. Repetition and simplicity of line play a large part in the construction of blues improvisations. This Fastline exemplifies this ideal as it contains only two notes. Keep a constant vibrato going during all the repetitions of the C crotchets.

FASTLINE Twenty Tempo: 60
Scale used: A blues.
Tech./harmonic aspects: Half/full tone bends.
Comments:
1. The final line includes repeated notes and emphasises the flattened fifth of the blues scale.

FASTLINES SOLO

FASTLINE BLUES PRIMER SOLO

Tempo: 60

The Fastline solo contains most, if not all, of the techniques outlined in the line by line section. Several Fastlines have been lifted directly out of lick section and alterations to existing lines have been made then placed in the solo. New ideas have also been added throughout. For more details about the Fastline solo and how to get the best out of it, turn to the projects section found later in this book. *To play along with just the backing chords of the solo, pan the speakers left/right.*

Intro bar: Contains the beginning of Fastline thirteen which is transposed down a major fourth.
Bars 2-3: Listen carefully to the recording of the solo if you encounter difficulty when exececuting this line due to rhythmic complexity.
Bars 4-5: The pick-up notes into bar five are the same as Fastline fourteen, but transposed down a major second. Remember to play the first three eighth notes in bar five staccato.
Bar 6: This bar contains a repetition of the phrase found in bar five.
Bar 7: The rake to the pull-off from C natural to A has to be played with one downward movement of the pick.
Bar 10: Ensure that you actually bend the E note up a minor third interval to a G note, slowly releasing downward while playing the phrase rhythmically correct.
Bar 12-13: As you finish the solo, play a *Rall.* (slow down) as you play the last four notes.

BACKING TRACKS

FASTLINE BLUES PRIMER BACKTRACK 1   Style: Medium Shuffle - Tempo 132

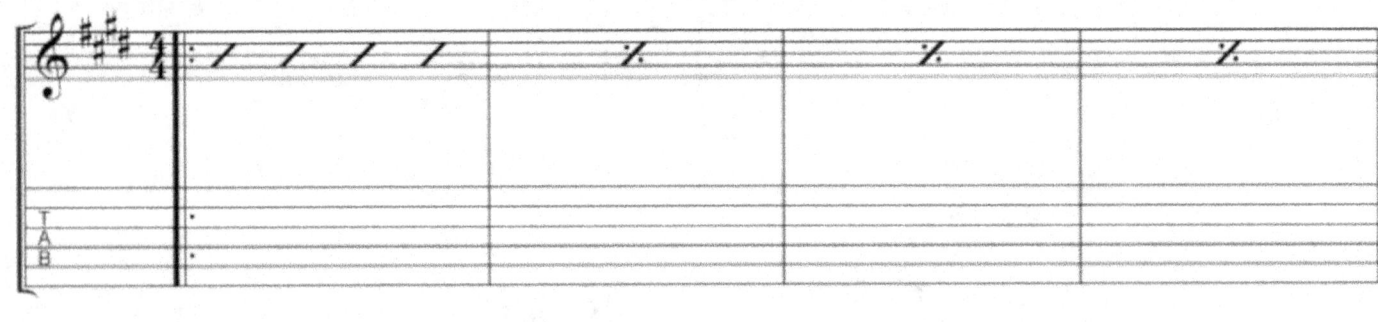

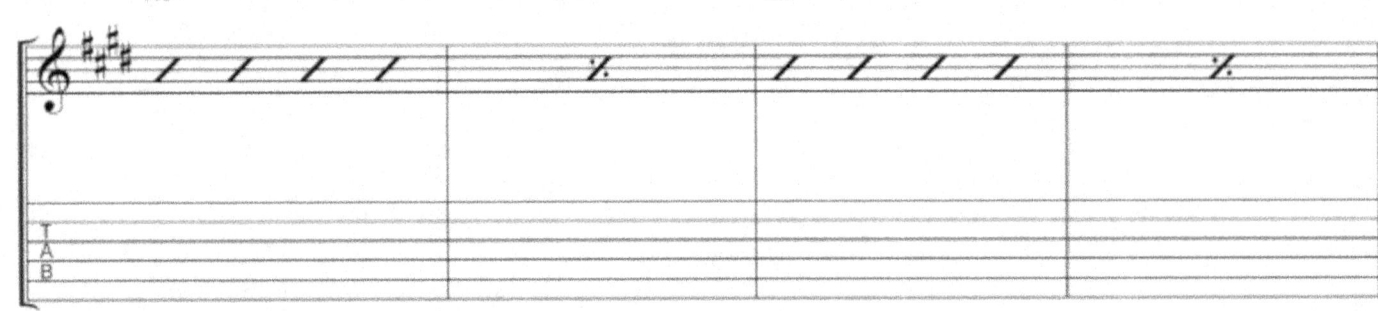

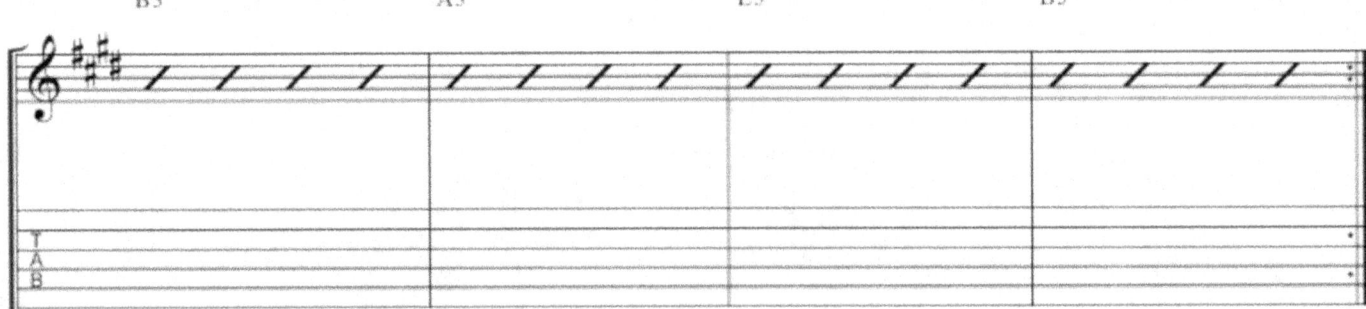

FASTLINE BLUES PRIMER BACKTRACK 2   Style: Slow Blues - Tempo 60

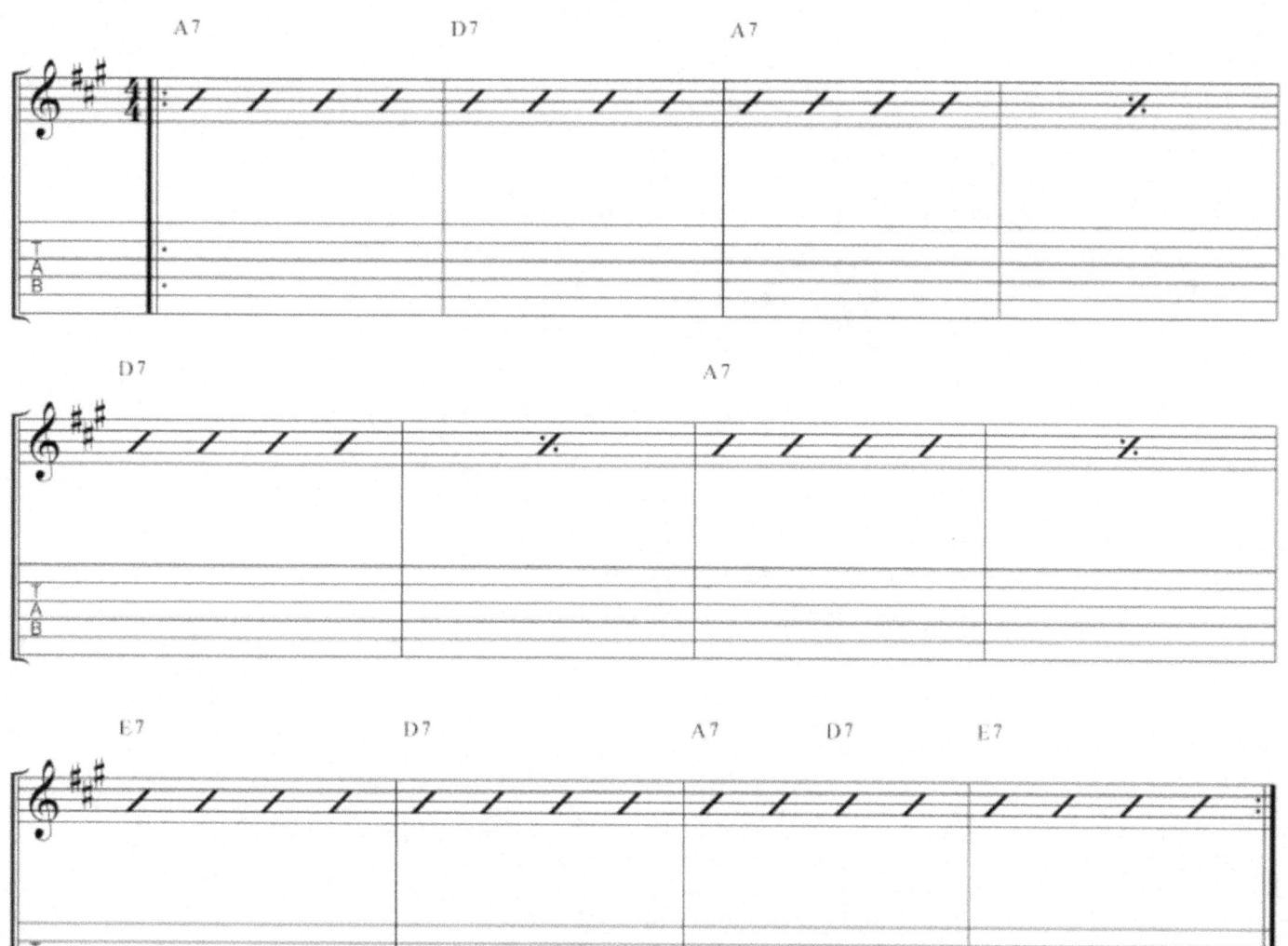

FASTLINE BLUES PRIMER BACKTRACK 3 Style: R&B - Tempo 176

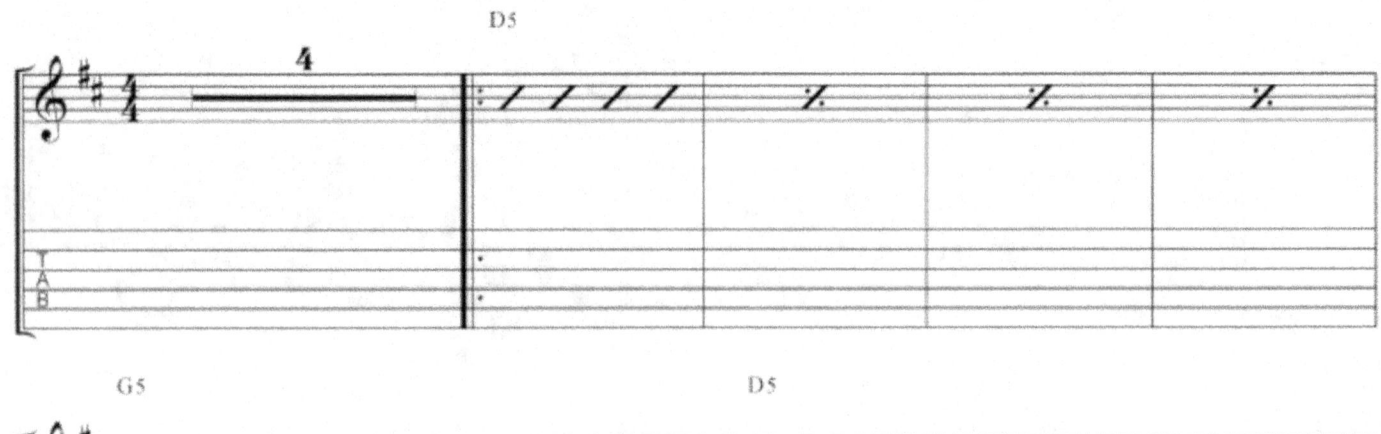

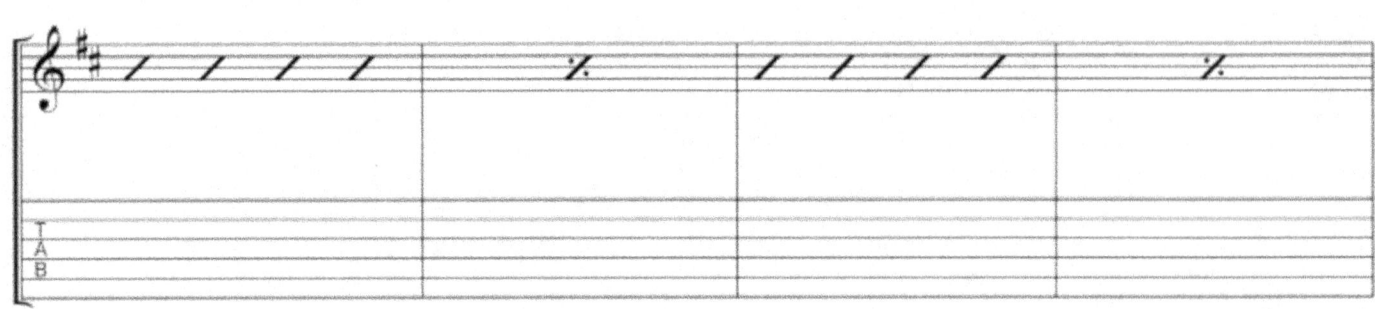

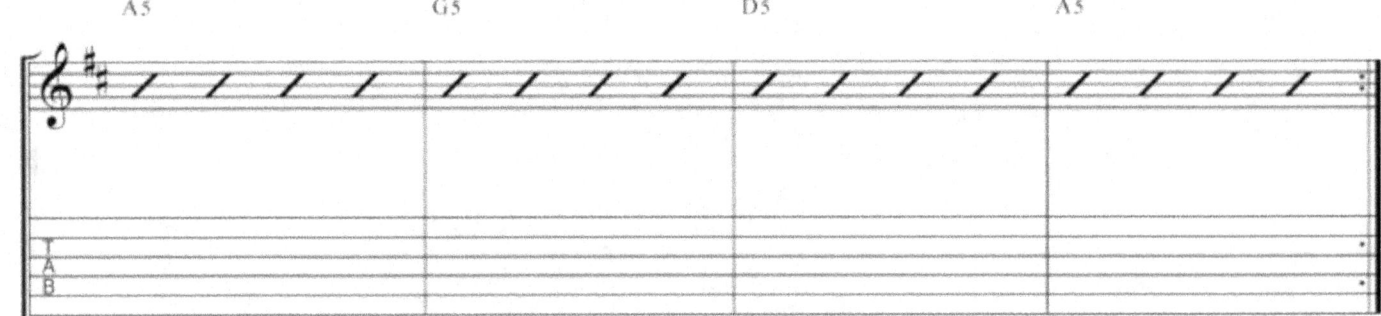

FASTLINE BLUES PRIMER BACKTRACK 4

Style: Shuffle & Stops - Tempo 126

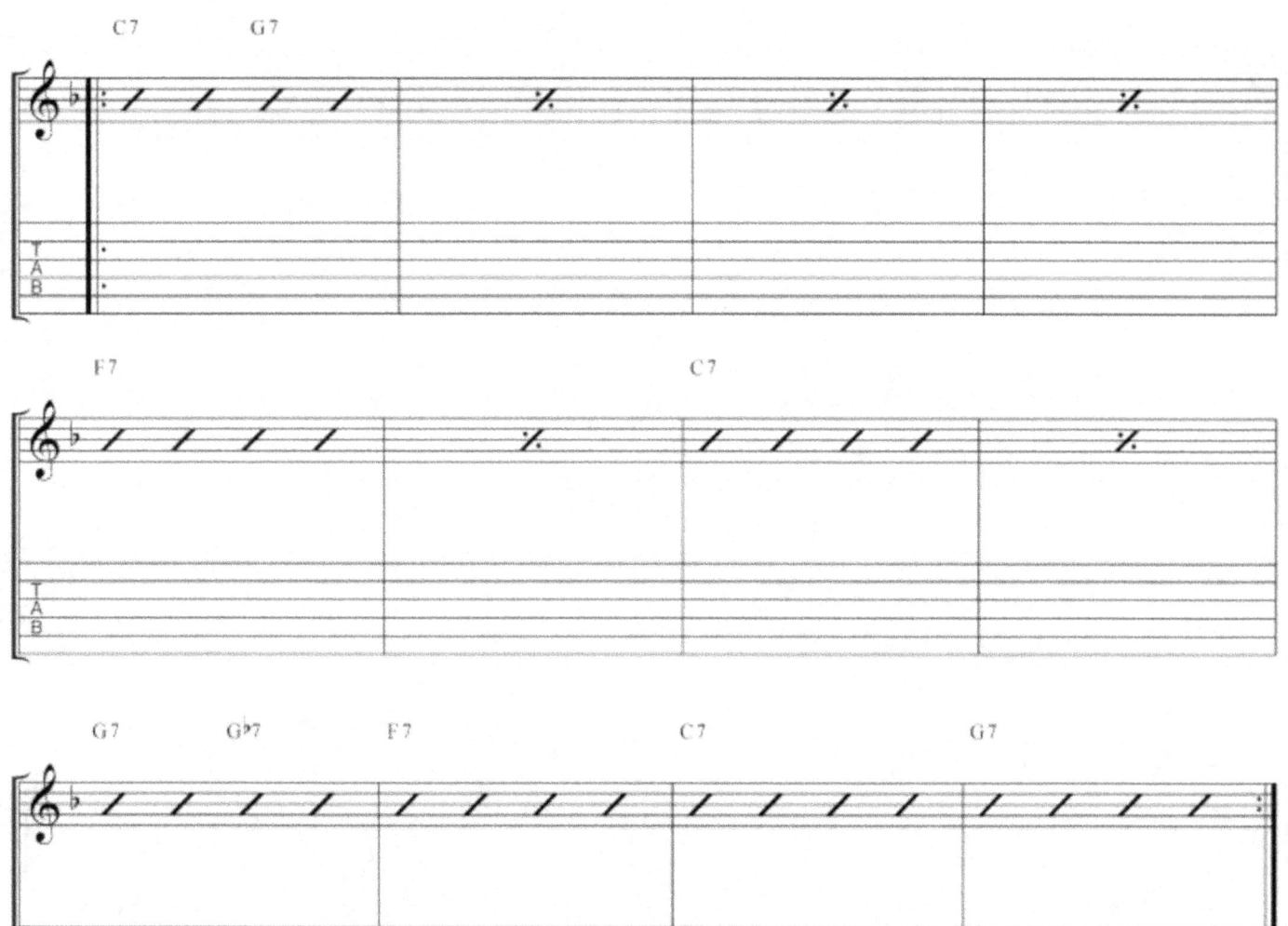

FASTLINE BLUES PRIMER BACKTRACK 5 Style: Walking Bass - Tempo 136

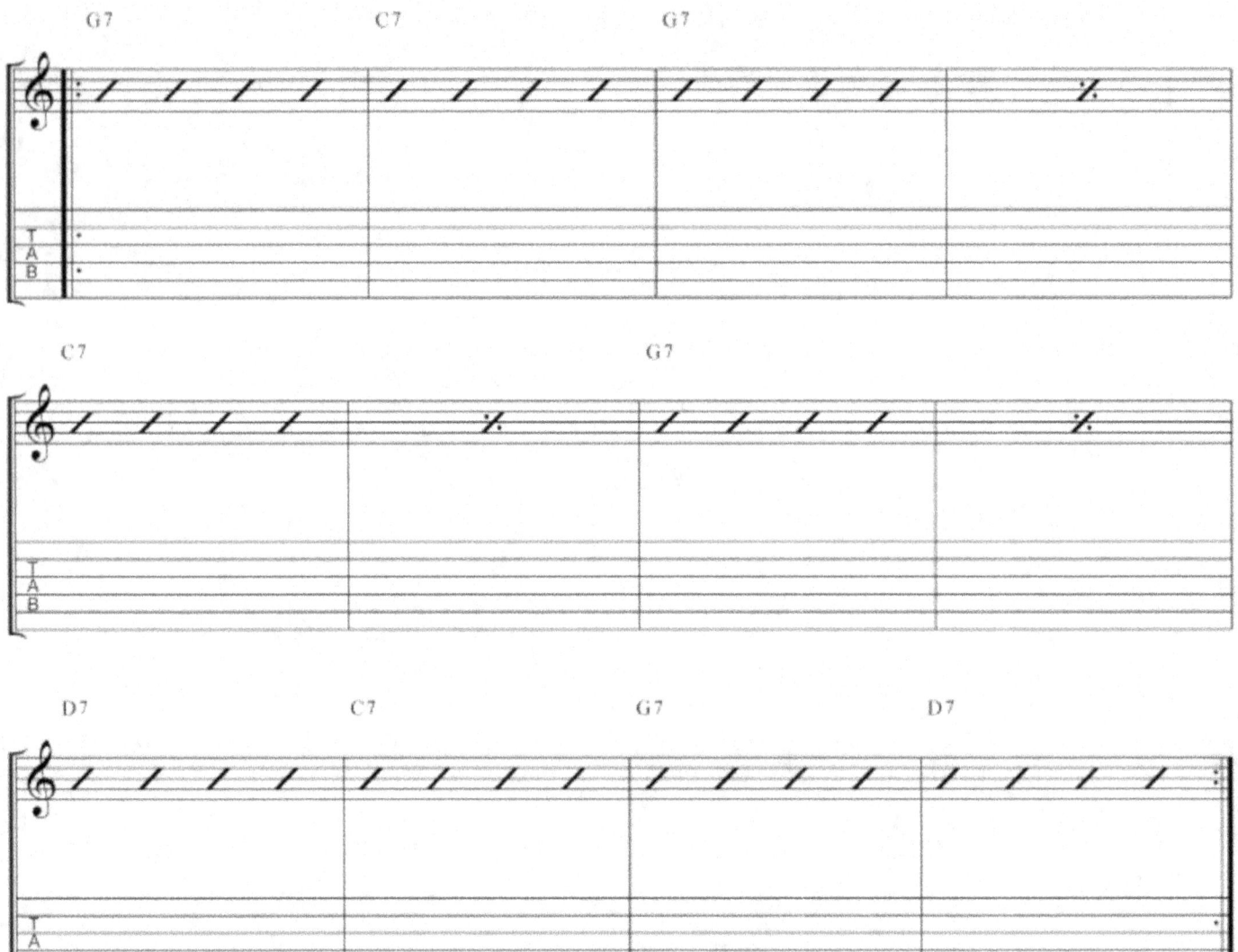

FASTLINE PROJECTS

FASTLINES BLUES PRIMER PROJECTS

Twelve bar blues progressions

This project is about developing the ability to play the blues in many different key signatures. A basic twelve bar blues progression is shown in the key of E in the Fastlines section.

Memorise the sound and movement of each chord in this progression, then work out the same sounds and movements relative to each chord in all new keys. The chords used are I, IV and V from a diatonic major chord system (triadic). Any new blues progression will keep this template of chords. For example, a twelve bar blues progression in the key of A would comprise of the chords A7 (chord I), D7 (chord IV) and E7 (chord V).

Start by working out the chords I, IV and V in the keys of D, G and A. The dominant seventh chords that you have to choose from are A7, D7, G7, E7 and C7. Remember, when you are trying to figure this out, keep the original chord movement sounds in your head.

Major and minor pentatonics

The three primary scales in blues guitar playing are the major pentatonic, minor pentatonic and blues scale, therefore a good understanding of the layout of these scales across the neck is essential. This can be done by learning the five pentatonic scale patterns.

As a minor pentatonic scale also doubles up as a major pentatonic scale through relative major/minor theory (and vica versa for major to minor) you are actually learning two of the three scales when you learn any one of the major or minor patterns.

The third scale, the blues scale, is a minor pentatonic scale with an added note - the flattened fifth. In A minor pentatonic this would be an E flat note.

Riffs

An important facet of blues guitar playing is the use of riffs or repeated figures. Fastline twelve is an example of this. Using riffs in your playing will give your solos a more compositional and unified sound instead of just a handful of unconnected musical ideas.

Using Fastline twelve as your example, make up short riff ideas of your own incorporating them into your solos and songs. Don't be afraid to repeat your riff ideas through an entire chorus of a twelve bar sequence.

Primary blues scale

Using only one scale as your base material for your lead ideas could result in your solos sounding dull and predictable. To avoid this, begin using the three primary blues scales over a give blues progression. These primary blues scales will provide you with new positions and scalar patterns necessary to draw further inspiration from.

To begin with, try learning the relevant scales in one position of the fretboard. Try this example which would work for a twelve bar blues in A. Play pattern two fingered at the fifth position. You will now be playing the A blues scale over an A blues progression. Move down to the fourth position playing pattern three (starting the scale with your second finger over the fifth fret). This is the scale of A major pentatonic. All these scales would be valid as improvisational material when playing over an A blues.

Twelve bar blues progressions

This project is about developing the ability to play the blues in many different key signatures. A basic twelve bar blues progression is shown in the key of E in the Fastlines section.

Memorise the sound and movement of each chord in this progression, then work out the same sounds and movements relative to each chord in all new keys. The chords used are I, IV and V from a diatonic major chord system (triadic). Any new blues progression will keep this template of chords. For example, a twelve bar blues progression in the key of A would comprise of the chords A7 (chord I), D7 (chord IV) and E7 (chord V).

Start by working out the chords I, IV and V in the keys of D, G and A. The dominant seventh chords that you have to choose from are A7, D7, G7, E7 and C7. Remember, when you are trying to figure this out, keep the original chord movement sounds in your head.

Major and minor pentatonics

The three primary scales in blues guitar playing are the major pentatonic, minor pentatonic and blues scale, therefore a good understanding of the layout of these scales across the neck is essential. This can be done by learning the five pentatonic scale patterns.

As a minor pentatonic scale also doubles up as a major pentatonic scale through relative major/minor theory (and vica versa for major to minor) you are actually learning two of the three scales when you learn any one of the major or minor patterns.

The third scale, the blues scale, is a minor pentatonic scale with an added note - the flattened fifth. In A minor pentatonic this would be an E flat note.

Riffs

An important facet of blues guitar playing is the use of riffs or repeated figures. Fastline twelve is an example of this. Using riffs in your playing will give your solos a more compositional and unified sound instead of just a handful of unconnected musical ideas.

Using Fastline twelve as your example, make up short riff ideas of your own incorporating them into your solos and songs. Don't be afraid to repeat your riff ideas through an entire chorus of a twelve bar sequence.

Primary blues scale

Using only one scale as your base material for your lead ideas could result in your solos sounding dull and predictable. To avoid this, begin using the three primary blues scales over a give blues progression. These primary blues scales will provide you with new positions and scalar patterns necessary to draw further inspiration from.

To begin with, try learning the relevant scales in one position of the fretboard. Try this example which would work for a twelve bar blues in A. Play pattern two fingered at the fifth position. You will now be playing the A blues scale over an A blues progression. Move down to the fourth position playing pattern three (starting the scale with your second finger over the fifth fret). This is the scale of A major pentatonic. All these scales would be valid as improvisational material when playing over an A blues.

QR CODES & LINES

QR CODES

QR CODES FOR VIDEO ON YOUR PHONE OR TABLET!

FASTLINES intro and tuning up notes

The above image is a QR code. These have been provided so you don't need to turn on a computer and quickly hear the relevant audio on your mobile phone or tablet whilst at your music stand.

1. Download a QR code reader from Google Play or the Mac store. There are many free programs.

2. Once downloaded, open up the app and point at the QR code. The relevant mp3 will open for you to play.

3. We tried to embed QR codes beside each musical example, however, there were issues regarding the small size of the QR code as well as spacing and the relevant mp3 file being activated. These pages provide a list for you to refer to and use when studying a specific line, the solo or Backtracks.

QR code for Fastline 1 Blues Primer

QR code for Fastline 2 Blues Primer

QR code for Fastline 3 Blues Primer

QR code for Fastline 4 Blues Primer

QR code for Fastline 5 Blues Primer

QR code for Fastline 6 Blues Primer

QR code for Fastline 7 Blues Primer

QR code for Fastline 8 Blues Primer

QR code for Fastline 9 Blues Primer

QR code for Fastline 10 Blues Primer

QR code for Fastline 11 Blues Primer

QR code for Fastline 12 Blues Primer

QR code for Fastline 13 Blues Primer

QR code for Fastline 14 Blues Primer

QR code for Fastline 15 Blues Primer

QR code for Fastline 16 Blues Primer

QR code for Fastline 17 Blues Primer

QR code for Fastline 18 Blues Primer

QR code for Fastline 19 Blues Primer

QR code for Fastline 20 Blues Primer

QR code for Backtrack 1 Blues Primer

QR code for Backtrack 2 Blues Primer

QR code for Backtrack 3 Blues Primer

QR code for Backtrack 4 Blues Primer

QR code for Backtrack 5 Blues Primer

HAVE YOU DOWNLOADED YOUR AUDIO FILES YET?

1. Book owners should access mp3 files for this book at the following URL…This is NOT a necessary step if you just wish to use the QR codes provided in this book.

    http://www.guitarandmusicinstitute/audiobluesprm/

2. For security purposes and in an effort to try and keep piracy to a bearable level you will be asked three questions which relate to words found on pages within this book. You will also be asked for your name and email.

3. A compressed file containing all the mp3 files will be downloadable from a link contained within an email that will be sent to the email address you have stipulated on correct completion of the questions.

4. Make sure to check your spam folder regarding this email just incase nothing turn up within five to ten minutes.

5. Thank you for purchasing this book and supporting further publications from GMI, we really do appreciate it.

PLEASE REVIEW AND STAR RATE THIS BOOK

If you have found this book helpful in your guitar playing development, please take the time to give a review and give the book a star rating. We value your contribution and it helps us when creating more resources for guitarists around the world.

Thanks for your time. Please visit us at the following URL address:

http://www.guitarandmusicinstitute.com